Starting any new idea is always difficult... Original documentary film from remote antiquity showing the ingenious inventor of the first boat.

# ALI MITGUTSCH

# ALL ABOUT SHIPS

Translated by Noel Simon

**J. M. Dent & Sons Ltd**
London & Melbourne

Hundreds of thousands of years ago man first ventured upon the water. It was a very risky undertaking. The daring inventor could have been carried on an uprooted tree or a bundle of branches. At first his hands and broken branches were all he had to use as paddles.

Boats were not the invention of only a few people. Numerous types of boats were developed in different places and at different times. Improved tools and implements made more sophisticated construction possible, gradually leading to the establishment of an important shipbuilding industry. Merchant ships of every nation sailed the seas, and several small countries, or individual cities such as Venice, became rich and powerful — rich through commerce and trade, and powerful through their fleets of warships.

Constant improvement to the design and construction of ships, together with greater knowledge of navigation, encouraged voyages of discovery and the eventual circumnavigation of the world. Mastery of steampower and further refinement of navigational techniques heralded a completely new chapter in human history: the age of steam, leading to propulsion by engines and turbines. Coal was until recently the principal fuel; today it is usually oil. Whether atomic power or solar energy offer better propellants for ships remains a possibility that still has to be explored.

The modern ship has evolved from the dugout canoe. Lateral struts, which enabled the vessel to carry a larger load, gradually changed into planking. As these planks became constantly higher and thicker, the tree trunk from which the dugout was fashioned gradually became the ship's keel.

All primitive people with access to large trees have developed dugout canoes. The usual method of hollowing out the tree trunk was by burning with hot stones.

The cheapest type of rubber dinghy is a disused car tyre

Non-alcoholic drink

One-man reed boat

Bamboo pole

The forerunner of today's rubber dinghy was the inflated hide of some animal

Melons

Afghan peasant farmer loading melons

Neck
Legs

The shape of the animal is easily recognizable

Twin masts carrying the reed sail help improve stability

Assyrian life-jacket

Ancient boat used on the Tigris and Euphrates for transporting goods

This type of boat - known as a coracle - is used by Irish fishermen to this day.

Wooden frame

Leather

Indian reed boat made from bundles of reeds lashed together (Mexico)

Diameter 1-10 metres

Tarred canvas cover

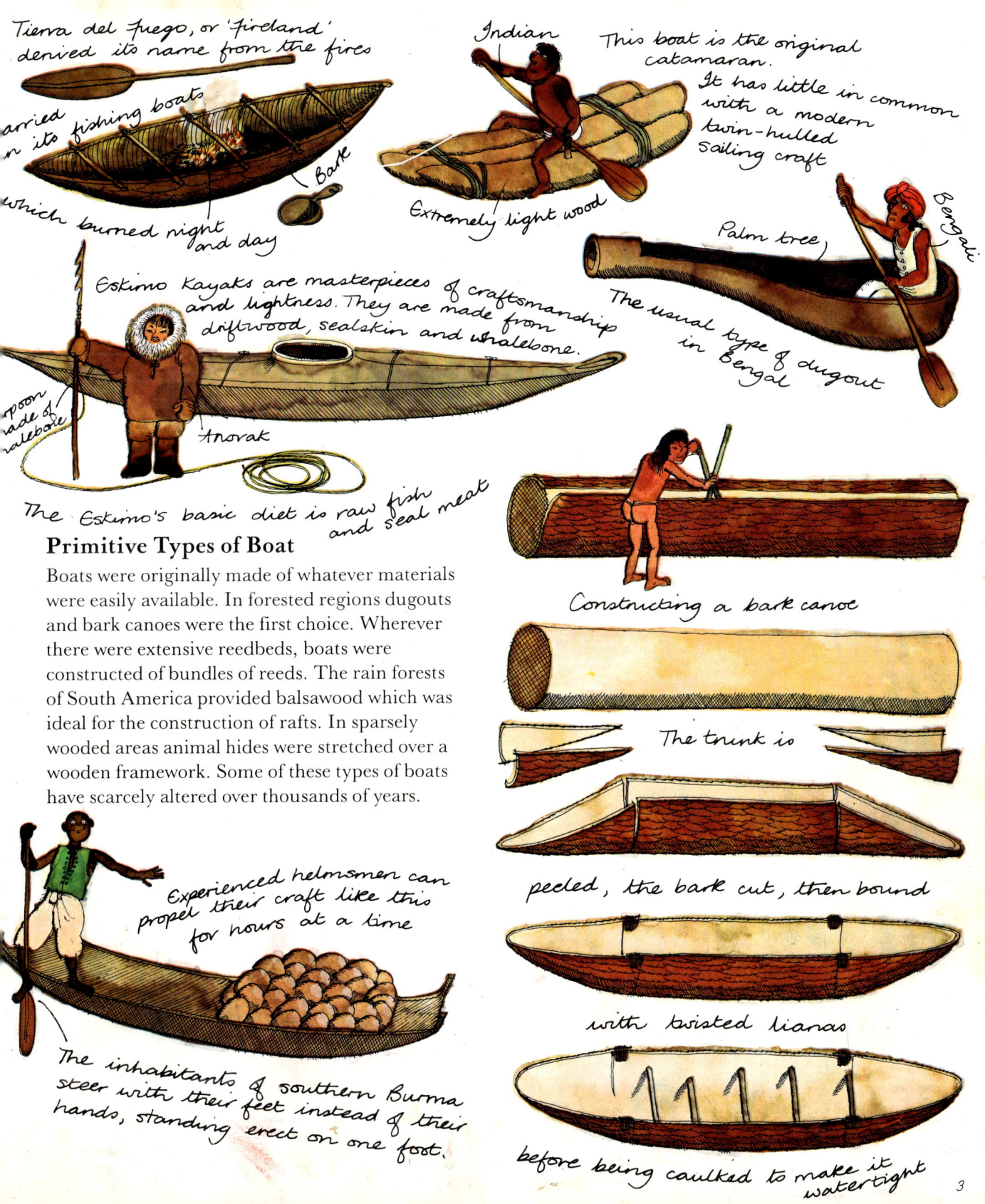

## Primitive Types of Boat

Boats were originally made of whatever materials were easily available. In forested regions dugouts and bark canoes were the first choice. Wherever there were extensive reedbeds, boats were constructed of bundles of reeds. The rain forests of South America provided balsawood which was ideal for the construction of rafts. In sparsely wooded areas animal hides were stretched over a wooden framework. Some of these types of boats have scarcely altered over thousands of years.

# Odysseus and Polyphemus

Odysseus and Polyphemus are characters from the Greek myths and legends. During his extensive voyaging, Odysseus and his companions reached the land of the one-eyed ogre, Polyphemus. After the giant had eaten one of his companions, Odysseus resorted to a trick to escape. He and his men made the ogre drunk and then blinded him. They then ran from the cave concealed in the thick wool of Polyphemus's sheep.

Odysseus had cunningly told his captor that his name was 'Nobody'. Thus, when Polyphemus cried, 'Nobody has blinded me. I shall kill nobody,' none of the other ogres came to his aid. And so Odysseus and his friends were able to escape.

*Richly decorated Chinese state junk used only on ceremonial occasions such as the visit of a friendly ruler.* — Silk flag — Sunshade — Dragon's head — Official — Helmsman — Stroke — Dragon's tail

*Arab dhow* — *Sinbad the Sailor and his companions* — Ship from the Pirate Coast

## Seafarers of the Pacific Ocean

The history of navigation in the Pacific Ocean goes back a long way and has included some remarkable seafarers. Among them are nomadic seamen who spent their entire lives at sea. Their vessels which look so frail are in reality the product of great knowledge and craftsmanship. Polynesian and Melanesian sailors, equipped only with primitive charts, navigated themselves with astonishing accuracy across thousands of miles of open sea.

*Steering position* — *Japanese junk* — *Bulwark* — A difficult boat to sail

*An armoured Korean warship known as a 'turtle'.* — Entrance — Dragon's head

## Noah's Ark

When God saw that mankind had strayed from the paths of righteousness and had neglected his commandments, he became extremely angry and resolved to destroy the whole of creation. But he saw that Noah alone was an honest and hard-working man, so commanded him:

'Build an ark and go aboard. Take your entire family with you. Also of every kind of animal take a pair, male and female, to ensure that living things shall be preserved upon earth. I shall cause rain to fall upon the earth for forty days and forty nights, and all other life shall perish.'

And it came to pass as God had said.

The only survivors of the flood were Noah and his immediate family and the animals he took with him into the ark.

# Seamonsters and Phantom Ships

Throughout the ages oceanic voyages have always involved great risk. Violent storms and unknown natural phenomena gave rise to stories of fantastic seamonsters and ghostly apparitions. All seafaring peoples are superstitious and relate tales of terrifying phantoms. Anyone, for instance, who whistled at sea could be severely punished, because his whistling was thought to mock the spirits of the storm. The legend of the 'Flying Dutchman' tells of a ghost ship that was condemned to sail the seas as a perpetual outcast.

## Viking Longboats

For more than two hundred years the Vikings and their longboats were the terror of the seas. They overran and ravaged the ports of northern and western Europe. The alarm cry 'the Northmen are coming' soon echoed around the shores of the Mediterranean and even as far as the Black Sea. The Vikings penetrated far inland by sailing up rivers: they plundered Paris, and their ships crossed Russia by river. They even explored the coast of Africa as far as the mouth of the Congo River.

In those days, around the year 1000, the climate of the northern hemisphere was milder than today. That was why the Vikings were able to settle briefly in Greenland from where they went on to discover North America. Their open boats gave no protection against rain and wind. This explains why the bold and warlike seafarers of old suffered badly from rheumatism. The helm was usually positioned on the right-hand side of the ship, to this day known as the 'starboard' side.

What sort of people were these Vikings? They were stockily built, usually had auburn or fair hair, and were regarded as ferocious fighters. Robbery, plunder, and slaughter became the Viking way of life.

Because of its light construction there was no difficulty in 'back-packing' a canoe around fast flowing rivers or from one stretch of water to another.

*Worried bird*

*Quarry*

To avoid the possibility of being mistaken for the enemy by their own kindred the figure-head was removed on the homeward journey.

The shape of the sail was designed not for beauty but because the Vikings did not know how to weave material other than in narrow widths.

The boat was steered by a rudder on the starboard side aft

## The Hanseatic Cog

The gradual withdrawal of the Viking conquerors towards the end of the 12th century, created conditions which permitted sea-borne trade to flourish. Certain leading ports in Germany and neighbouring countries formed an alliance aimed at mutual protection. This was the origin of the powerful Hanseatic League. The League encouraged commercial expansion which, in turn, called for the building of much larger vessels, notably the broad-beamed cog. This ship was no longer steered from the side but from the stern.

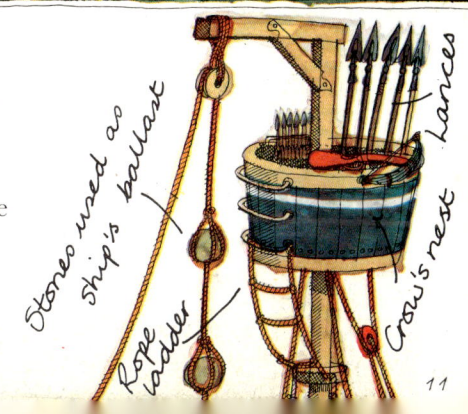

Stones used as ship's ballast

Rope ladder

Lances

Crow's nest

Clock or hour-glass used in fixing the position of the stars

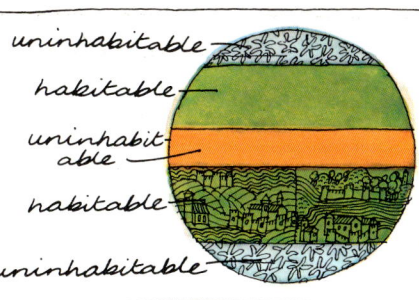

uninhabitable
habitable
uninhabitable
habitable
uninhabitable

This extract from a Portuguese book published in 1509 shows the general ignorance about the habitable parts of the world.

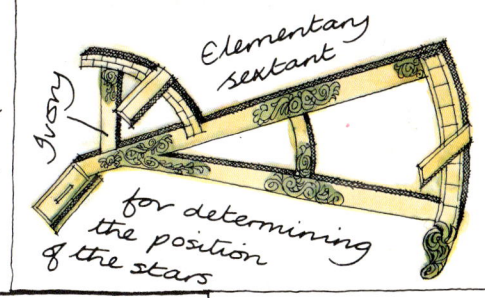

Elementary sextant — Ivory — for determining the position of the stars

Columbus promised a rich reward to the first man to sight foreign land. But he tricked him out of his reward.

Main sail

Bowsprit

Plumbing the depth of the water

## The Age of Discovery

The early seafarers had already mastered the art of determining the whereabouts of their ship from the position of the stars. The magnetic compass had been in use for about seven hundred years. Improved navigational techniques and the urge to explore were both encouraged by the belief that the earth was not a flat disc but a sphere.

In 1492, Christopher Columbus set sail with three Spanish ships to discover a new sea route to India. He had difficulty in finding a crew to man his ships from among the superstitious seamen of the day, and therefore had to make do with convicts, dragooned into service by the promise of being granted their freedom on their return.

Columbus landed in America but, until his dying day, he remained convinced that he had in fact reached India. The success of his historic voyage encouraged other adventurers to undertake further voyages of discovery. New sea routes were thus opened and unknown parts of the world discovered. These early explorers were soon followed by conquerors who annihilated entire peoples. Their ships brought great sorrow to the New World.

In 1519 Ferdinand Magellan became the first man to sail around the world

Magellan, a Portuguese adventurer, employed by Spain, was killed by natives in the Philippines; his voyage was completed by his senior surviving officer.

Canvas was spread on deck to collect rain water

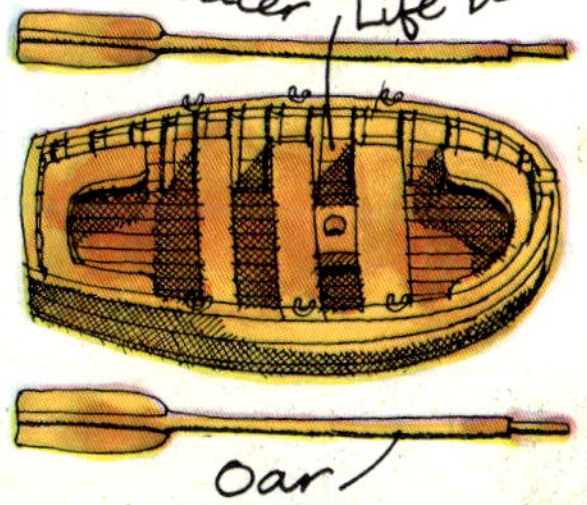

Life boat

Oar

A rogues' gallery of freebooters and pirates over the centuries

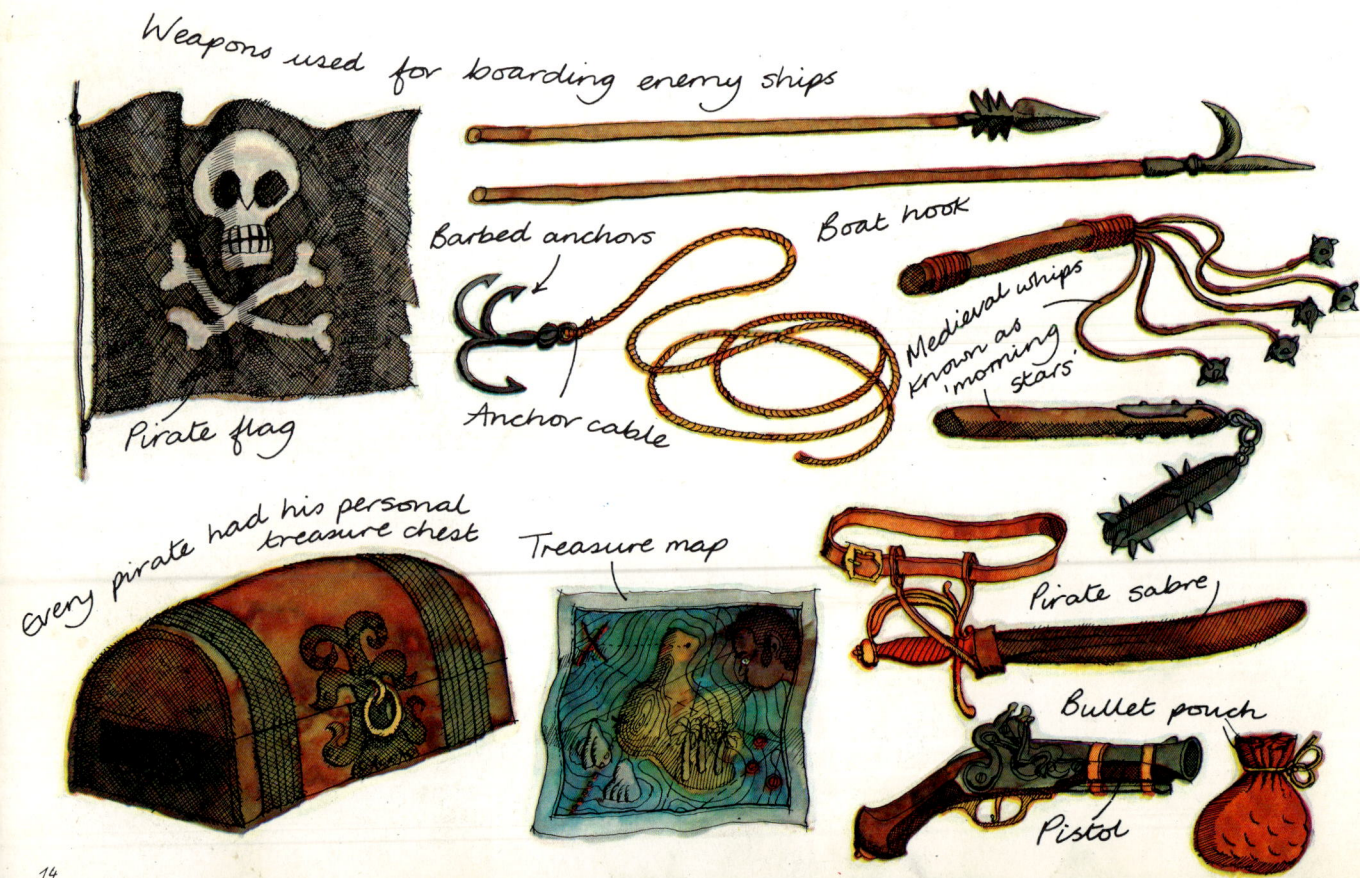

Weapons used for boarding enemy ships

Pirate flag

Barbed anchors

Boat hook

Anchor cable

Medieval whips known as 'morning stars'

Every pirate had his personal treasure chest

Treasure map

Pirate sabre

Pistol

Bullet pouch

permits stating that they were not outlaws but free and respectable citizens of the country in question. In return they had to swear to confine their attacks to enemy ships only. This system made it possible for many a cruel freebooter to live to enjoy a comfortable and prosperous old age.

An unpleasant end was nevertheless meted out to the German pirate Klaus Störtebeker and his accomplices, executed in Hamburg in 1402. To ensure that after he was beheaded his accomplices should not go free and get away with his ill-gotten gains, Störtebeker betrayed them one by one and went to his own death only after the fourteenth and last of his erstwhile comrades had been executed.

## Pirates in Swift Ships

Ever since ships began carrying rich cargoes and treasure there have also been robbers ready to waylay them. The Pirate Coast is a stretch of land in the northeastern part of the Arabian Peninsula, a name by which it is still known. If they believed themselves strong enough pirates would sometimes even attack ports and towns. Their arrival heralded an orgy of robbery and mindless destruction: everything would be plundered and laid waste. Countries at war with one another sometimes encouraged pirates to fight for them. The pirates would be given

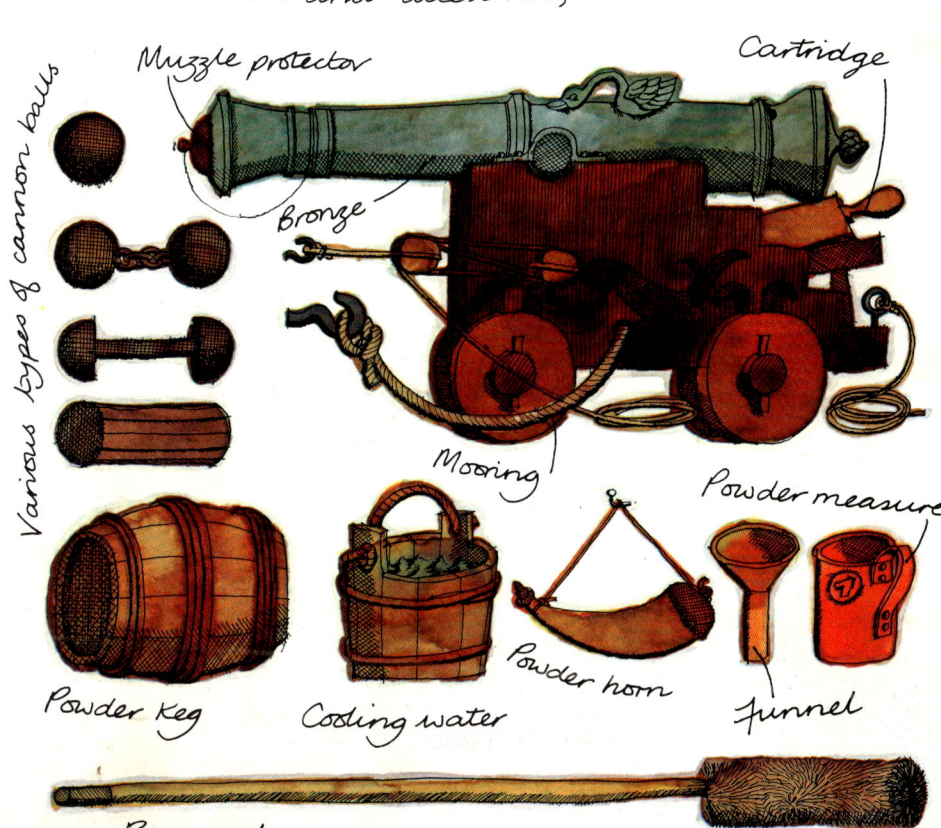

## Unwilling Seamen

Greek as well as Roman galleys were originally crewed by volunteers — free men. But later it became the practice to man them with prisoners-of-war and convicts condemned to hard labour. They received no pay and, under the remorseless lash of the cat-o'-nine tails, were forced to work until they dropped.

The French and Venetian galleys of the late Middle Ages are regarded as among the most attractive vessels ever built. But their beautiful lines concealed from the onlooker the hardship that was basic to life aboard them. In severe seas the helmsman was often up to his waist in water. There were no sanitary facilities, for which reason the oarsmen's benches stank terribly. In wartime people were often condemned to the galleys for the smallest offence. In 1692, for example, a Frenchman was sentenced to ten years in the galleys for stealing two loaves.

Thwart, or seat, with five galley slaves to each oar

The oarsmen were seldom unchained, and then only to prolong their lives a little

Drum for beating time

Hammer

Slave

Stern lantern

Rudder

Layout of a slaving vessel

Below decks there was room neither to stand nor to lie down.

In storm or calm, up to three-quarters of the human cargo might perish

The human cargo was crammed so tightly into the holds that there was scarcely room to move.

*Log line and glass. The log was trailed astern of the vessel to measure the distance covered.*

*Slight bump* — *Extremely drunk* — *Press gang shanghaiing two young townsmen*

*Tough seaman of about 1810*

*Knots*

*Pipe*

*Seaman's pay (riches by nautical standards)*

*Tattooing lasts for ever*

*Lockable kitbag, highly decorated*

*Tattooing involves puncturing the skin with a fine needle which injects coloured dye.*

## Life under Sail

A seaman's life in the days of sail was hard and dangerous. After a storm, or if becalmed, the food, such as it was, usually went mouldy and became almost inedible. Everyone suffered from scurvy. In rain or storm the topsails had to be reefed or furled, often under appalling conditions. Such a life could be endured only by the dregs of society or those who had fallen foul of the law. For these reasons life on board was rough, coarse, and unpleasant in the extreme; discipline could be maintained only by the threat of severe punishment.

Good seamen were difficult to find. The perpetual shortage of seamen was met by the press gang: men were kidnapped from ale houses,

22

Ship's carpenter's tools

Brace — Mallet — Plumb line — Plane — Hatchet — Cobbler's tool

## Shipwrights at Work

Deck joists — Scaffolding — Deck planking — Stern timbers — Keel — Bottom planking

The so-called 'draw blade' was used for smoothing beams and baulks of wood, and trimming edges.

Planks sawn by hand — Heavy trestles — Frame saw

Baulks of timber were trimmed with axe or adze

No timber was ever wasted, however oddly shaped

A fire was used for bending planks into shape — Planks

Ladder for carrying some of the more awkward pieces

21

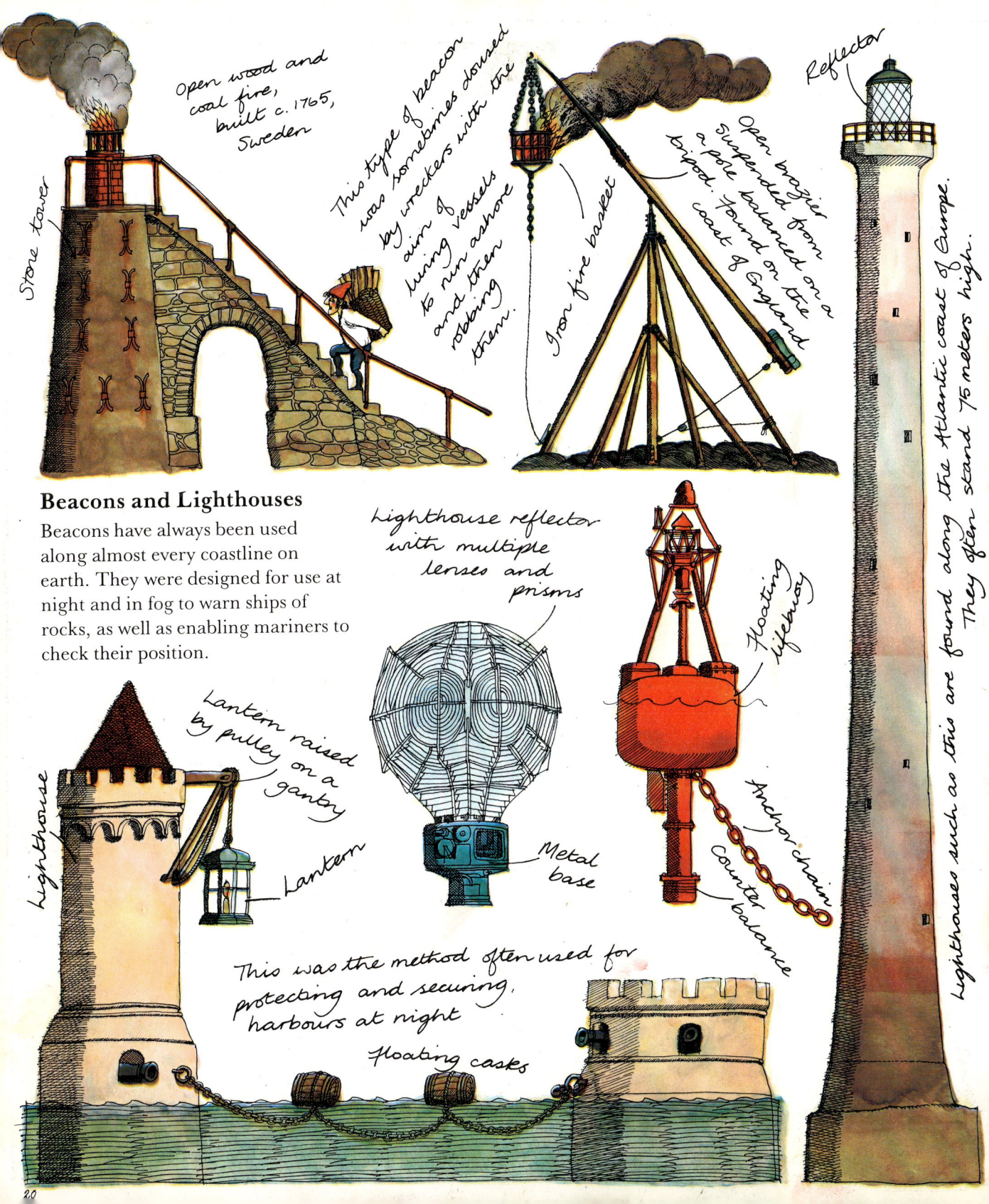

## Beacons and Lighthouses

Beacons have always been used along almost every coastline on earth. They were designed for use at night and in fog to warn ships of rocks, as well as enabling mariners to check their position.

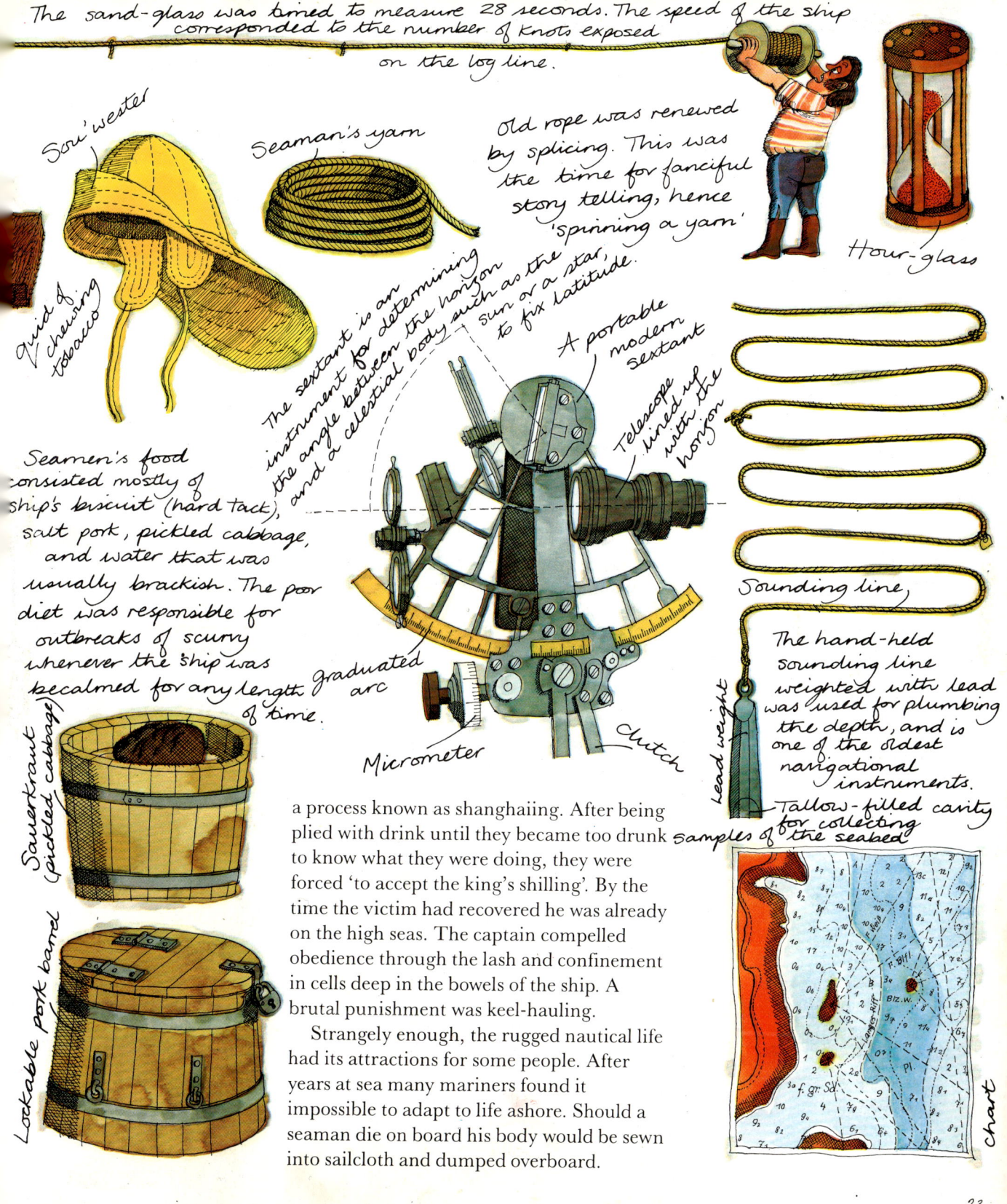

a process known as shanghaiing. After being plied with drink until they became too drunk to know what they were doing, they were forced 'to accept the king's shilling'. By the time the victim had recovered he was already on the high seas. The captain compelled obedience through the lash and confinement in cells deep in the bowels of the ship. A brutal punishment was keel-hauling.

Strangely enough, the rugged nautical life had its attractions for some people. After years at sea many mariners found it impossible to adapt to life ashore. Should a seaman die on board his body would be sewn into sailcloth and dumped overboard.

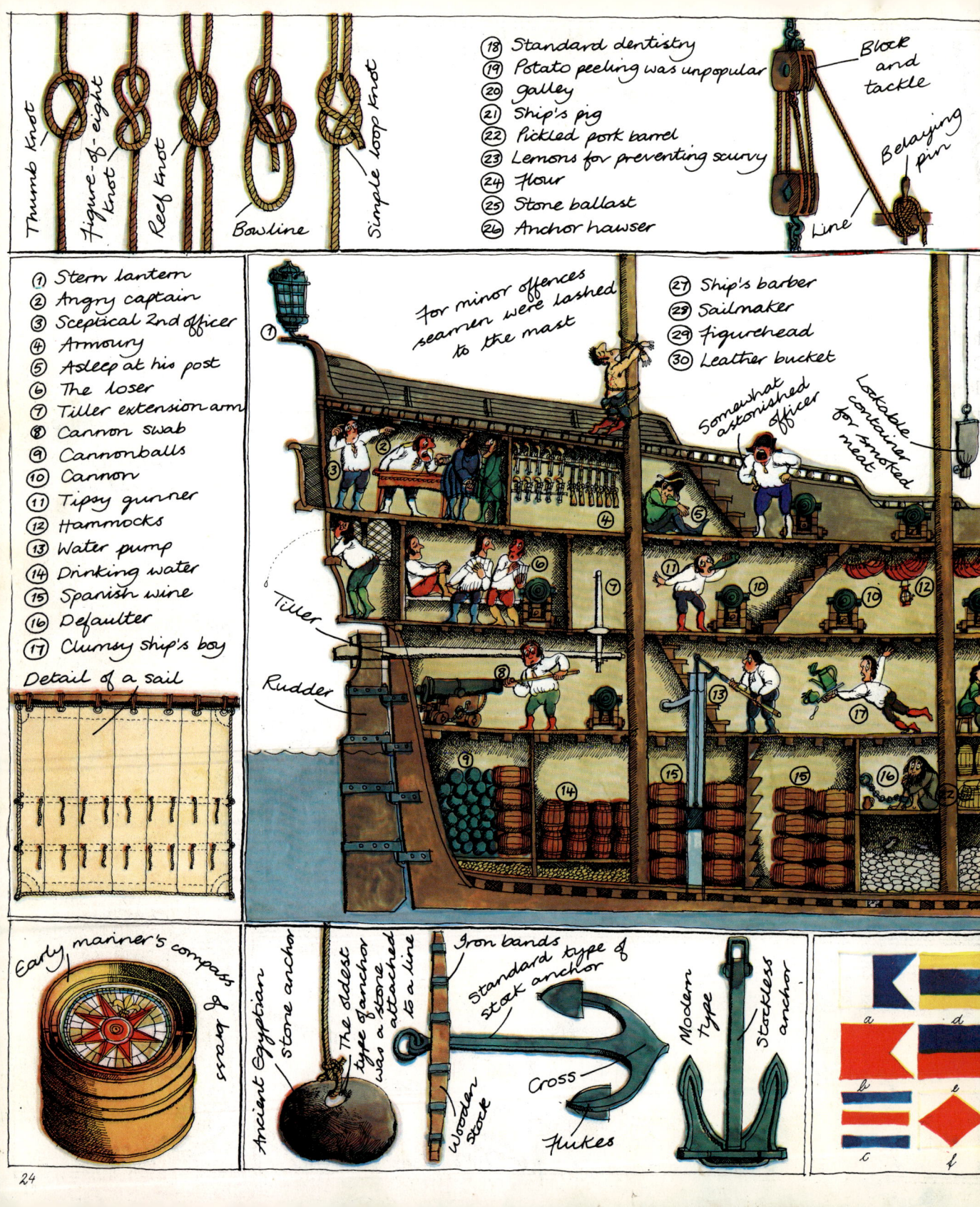

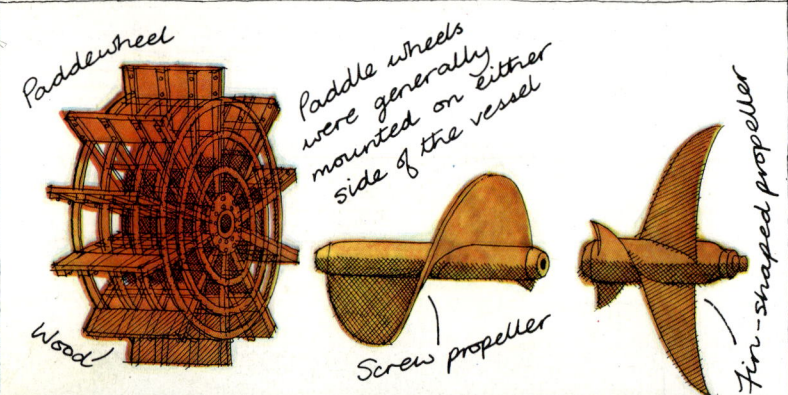

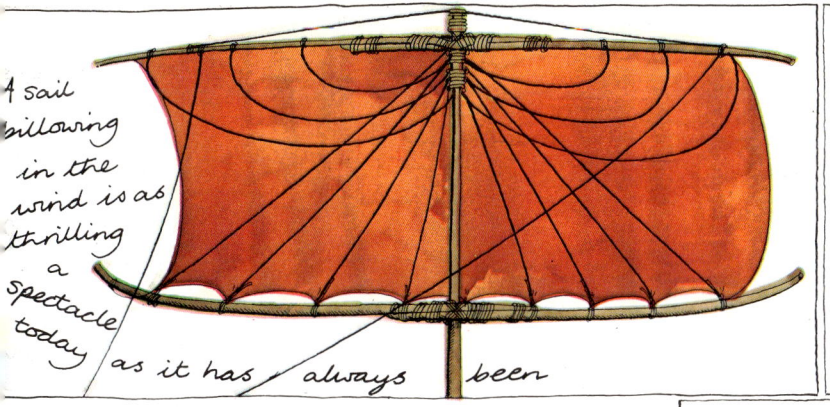
A sail billowing in the wind is as thrilling a spectacle today as it has always been

This is a picture of a medieval boat with hand-operated paddlewheels
Wooden paddlewheels

## Methods of Propulsion

Ever since the flat of the hand was first used to paddle, a means of propulsion through the water has always been a challenge. Early man had to be content with the paddle, oar or pole. Then he discovered how to take advantage of the power of the wind. Using sails of bark, fibre matting, wickerwork, linen or canvas, the wind was harnessed. A sailing vessel's dependence on the direction and strength of the wind was, of course, an important limitation. Constant improvements to the sails allowed better use to be made of the wind. In time man learned that by steering a zigzag course, it was possible to sail in any direction, including into wind.

The invention of the steam engine put an end to dependence on wind. Steamers could sail wherever they liked regardless of the wind. Many ingenious mechanical devices were invented and constantly improved with use. The methods of propulsion in use today are still in process of development and will very likely soon be changed and improved upon.

Steam paddle-boat designed by the American, John Fitch, in 1786

The 'Ernest Bazin' built in 1896
wheels

The 'Rattler' 200 h.p.
The 'tug-of-war' between paddlewheel and propeller was won by the propeller
The 'Alecto' 200 h.p.

27

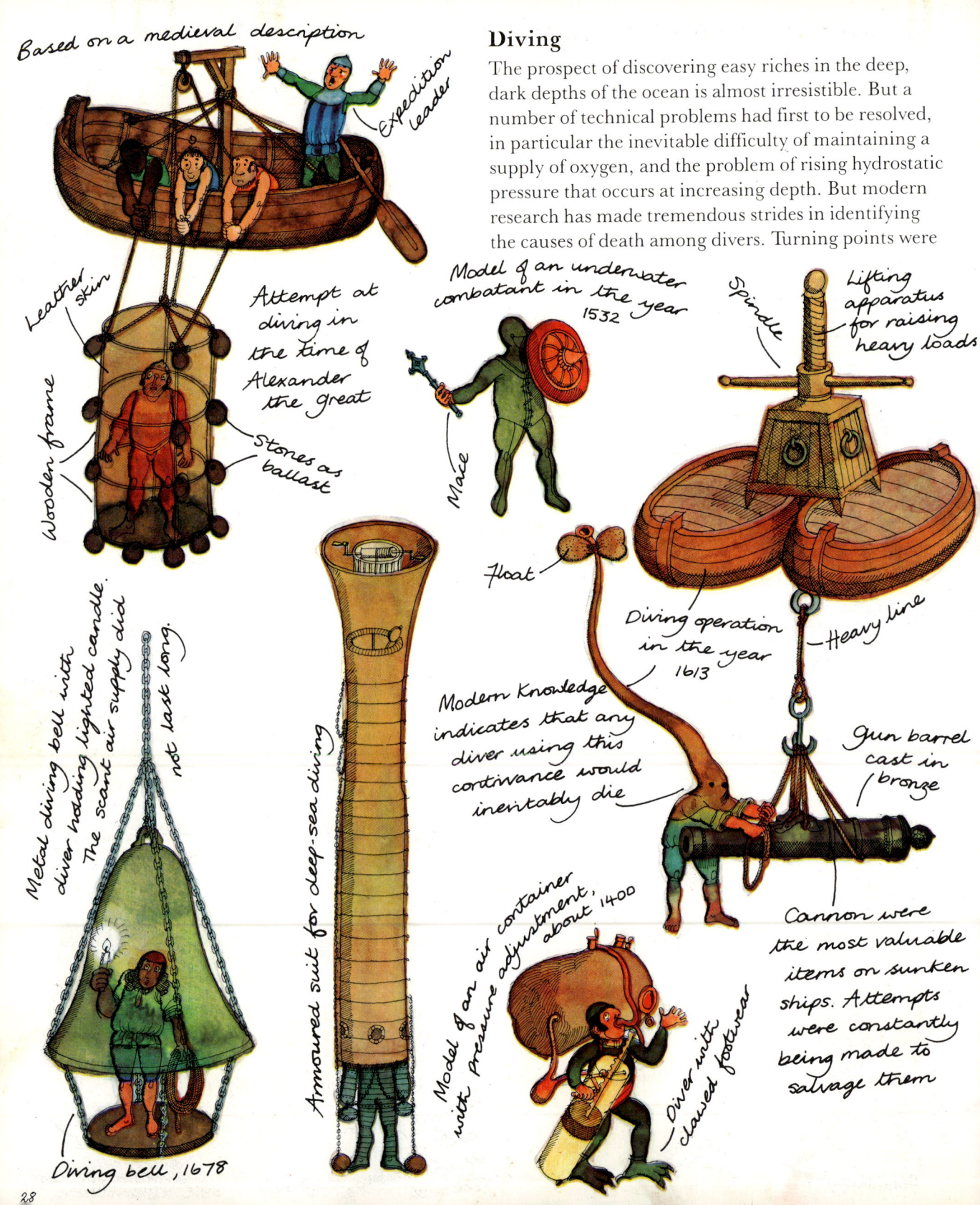

## Diving

The prospect of discovering easy riches in the deep, dark depths of the ocean is almost irresistible. But a number of technical problems had first to be resolved, in particular the inevitable difficulty of maintaining a supply of oxygen, and the problem of rising hydrostatic pressure that occurs at increasing depth. But modern research has made tremendous strides in identifying the causes of death among divers. Turning points were

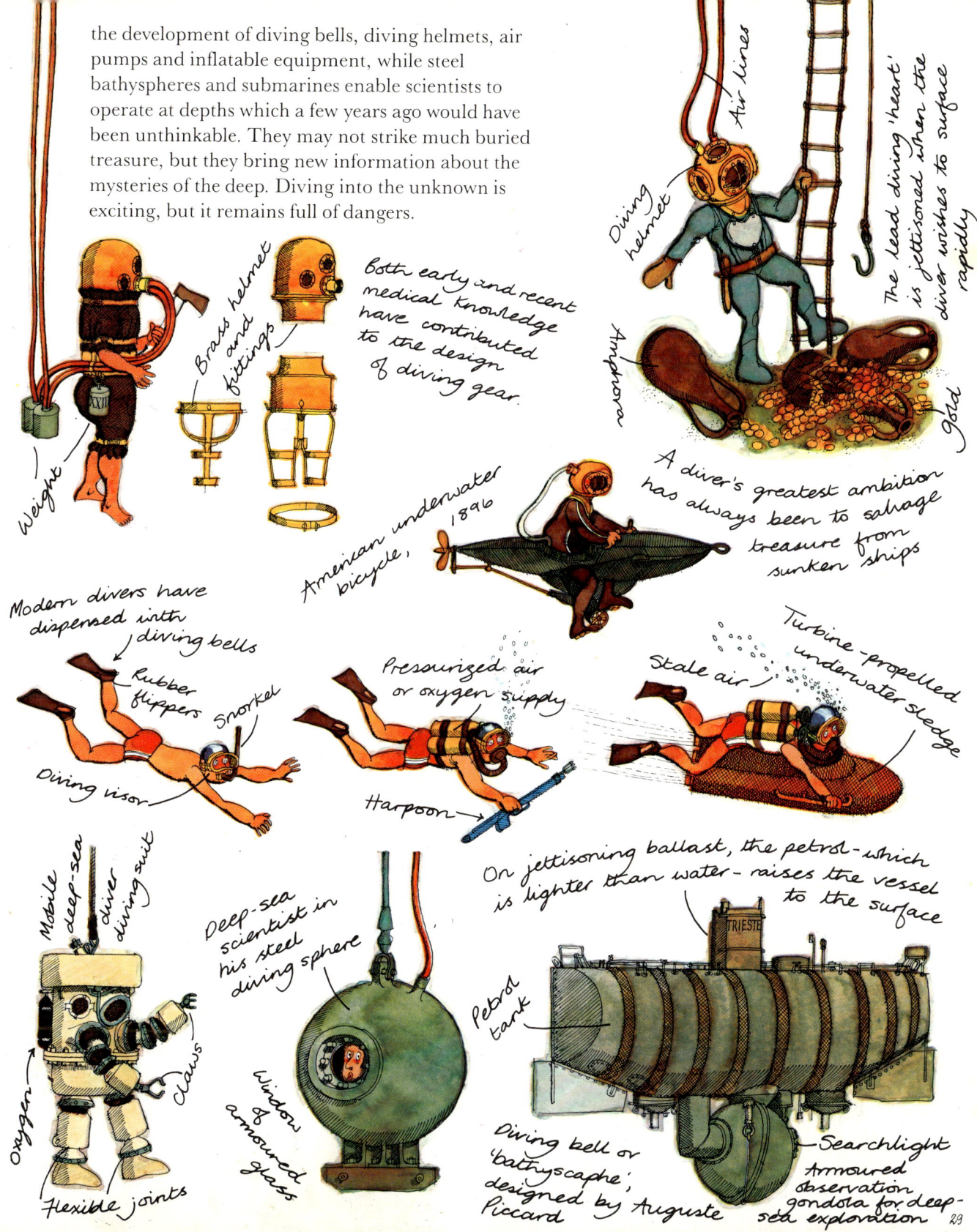

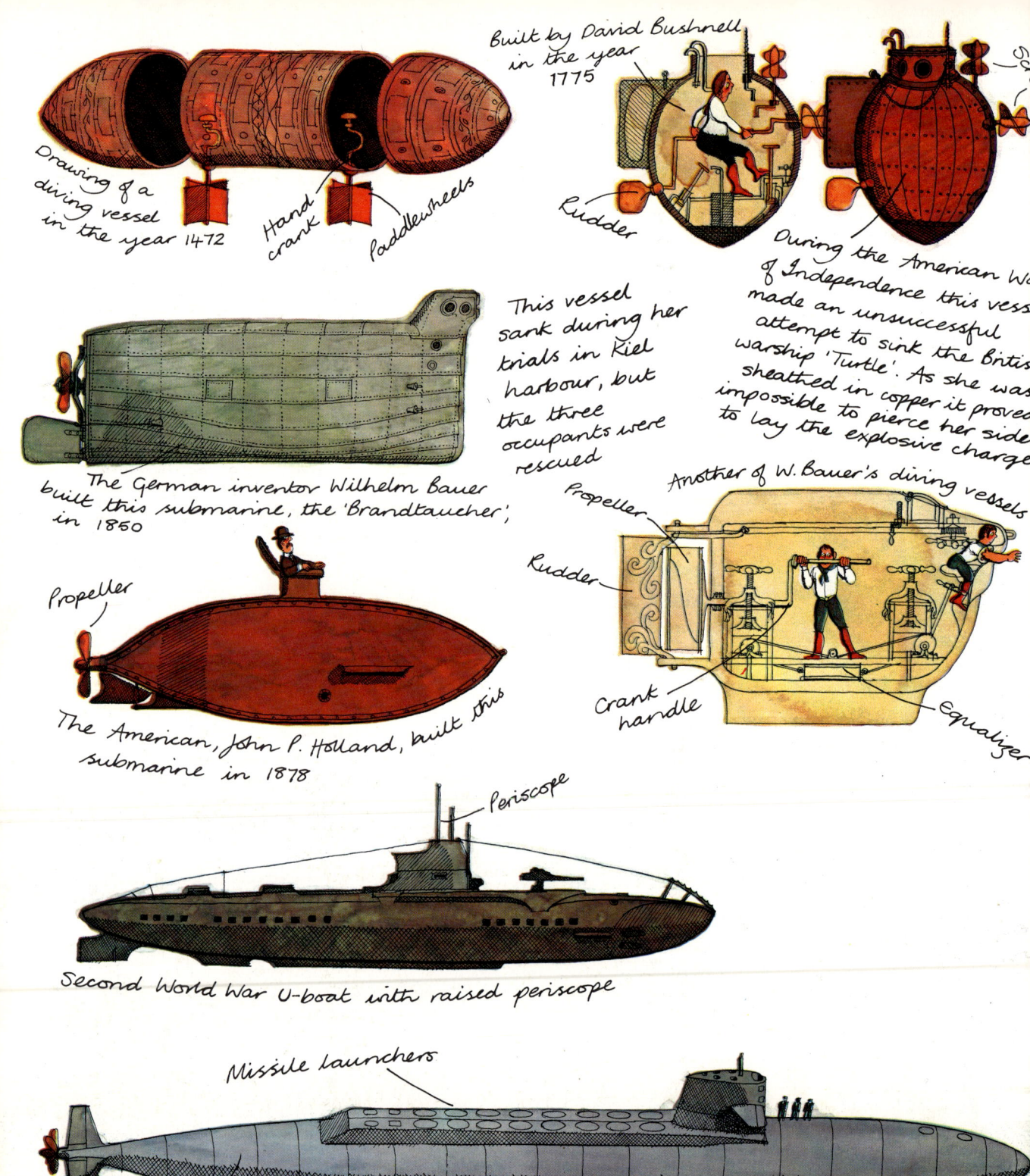

# River Boats

River-boat journeys have always been closely linked with sea voyages. Although the river boatman does not have to battle with gales or wrestle with being becalmed in the doldrums, he may well have to cope with shoal waters, rocks and whirlpools. The downstream journey is as a rule uneventful — as long as the river is not in flood. Upstream travel is usually more difficult and can make a lot of work. The river boat's shallow draft gives it the advantage of being able to go where sailing vessels could not, which explains why the paddle-steamer was chosen as the ideal vessel for rivers and lakes. It quickly became a familiar sight on large rivers and inland waters. The most renowned river steamers were built in America and operated on the Mississippi and Missouri rivers. Much larger steamboats were built for use on the open sea: in time steam came to take the place of sail.

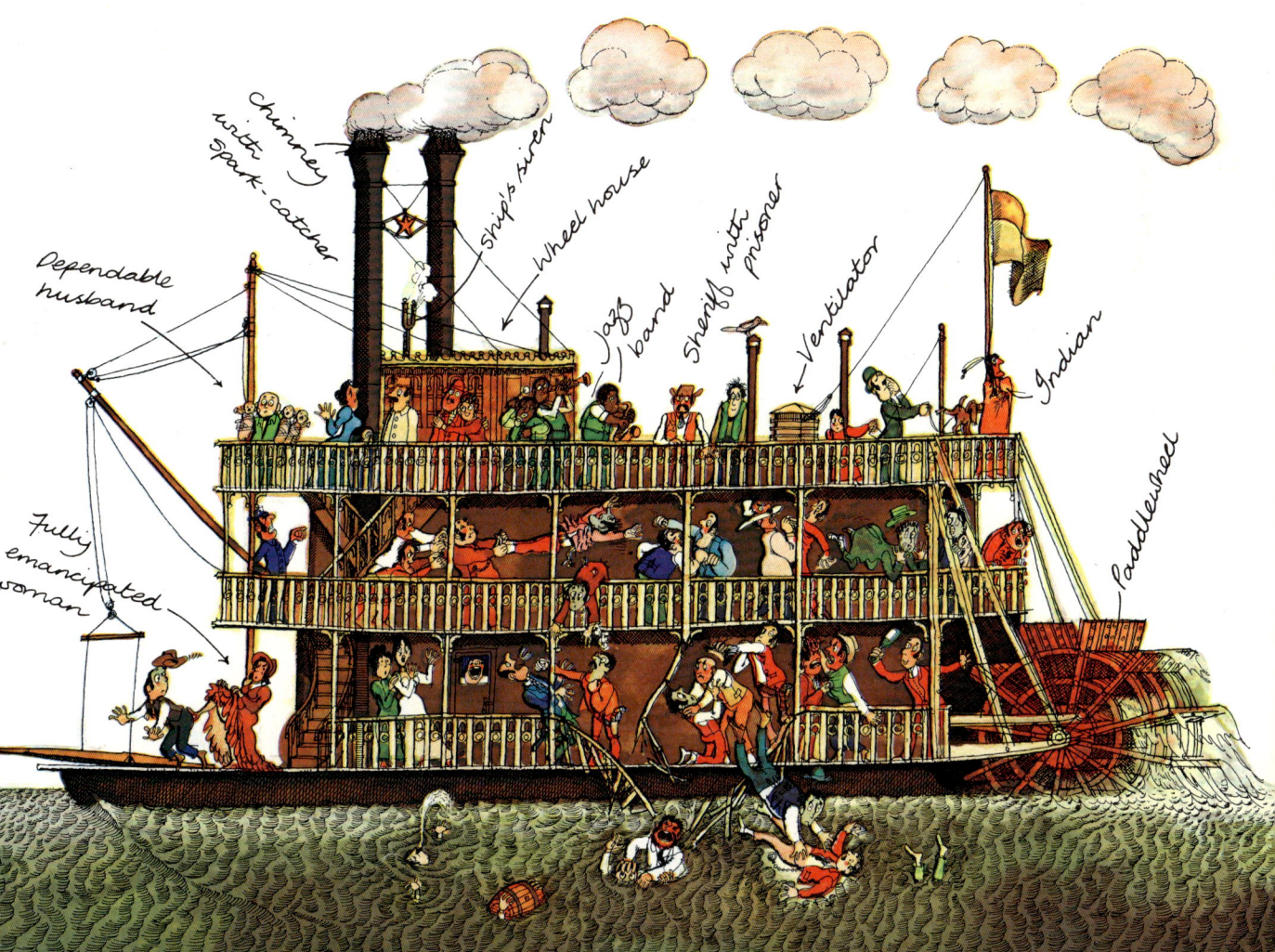

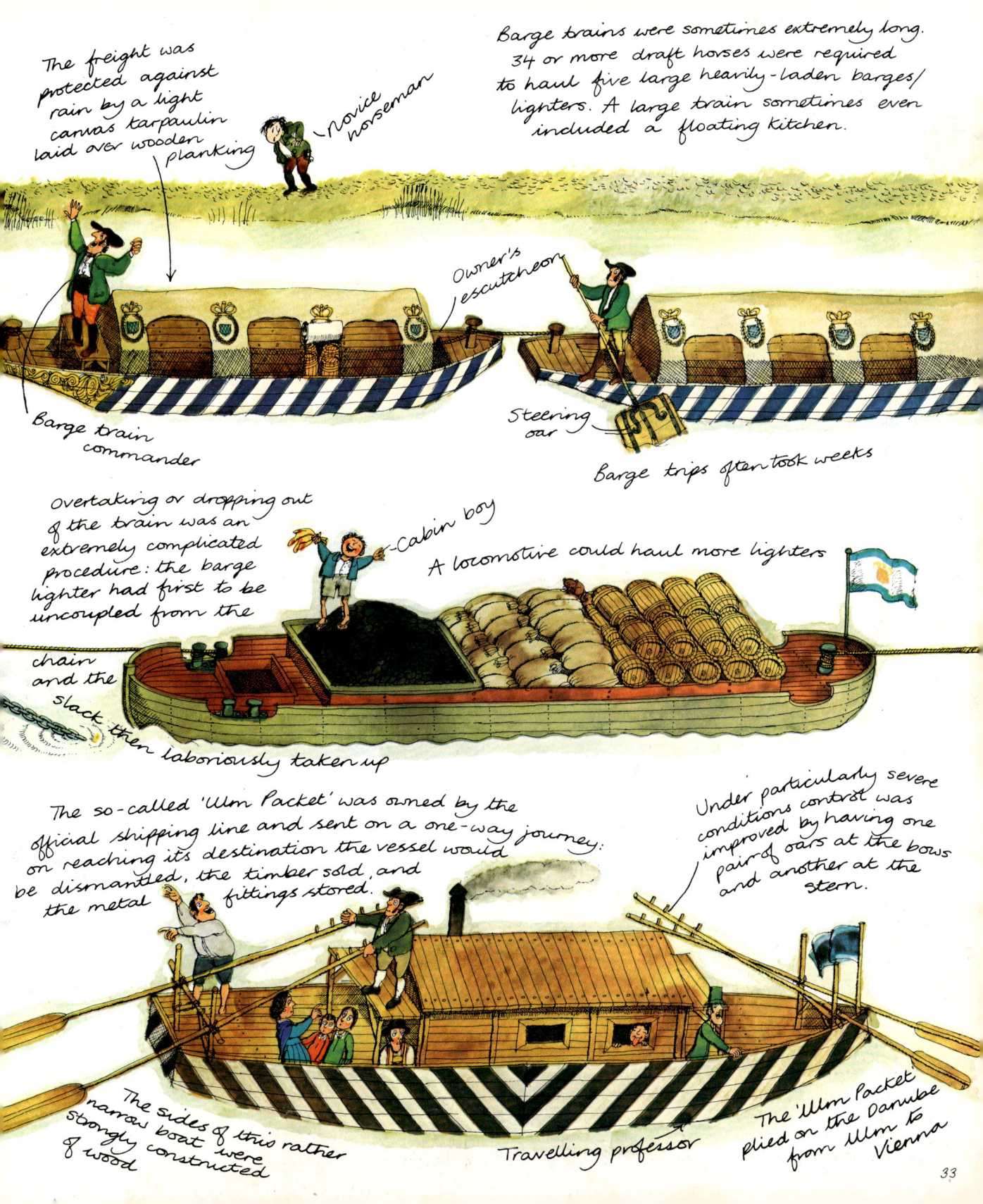

The freight was protected against rain by a light canvas tarpaulin laid over wooden planking

Novice horseman

Barge trains were sometimes extremely long. 34 or more draft horses were required to haul five large heavily-laden barges/lighters. A large train sometimes even included a floating kitchen.

Owner's escutcheon

Barge train commander

Steering oar

Barge trips often took weeks

Overtaking or dropping out of the train was an extremely complicated procedure: the barge lighter had first to be uncoupled from the chain and the slack then laboriously taken up

Cabin boy

A locomotive could haul more lighters

The so-called 'Ulm Packet' was owned by the official shipping line and sent on a one-way journey: on reaching its destination the vessel would be dismantled, the timber sold, and the metal fittings stored.

Under particularly severe conditions control was improved by having one pair of oars at the bows and another at the stern.

The sides of this rather narrow boat were strongly constructed of wood

Travelling professor

The 'Ulm Packet' plied on the Danube from Ulm to Vienna

33

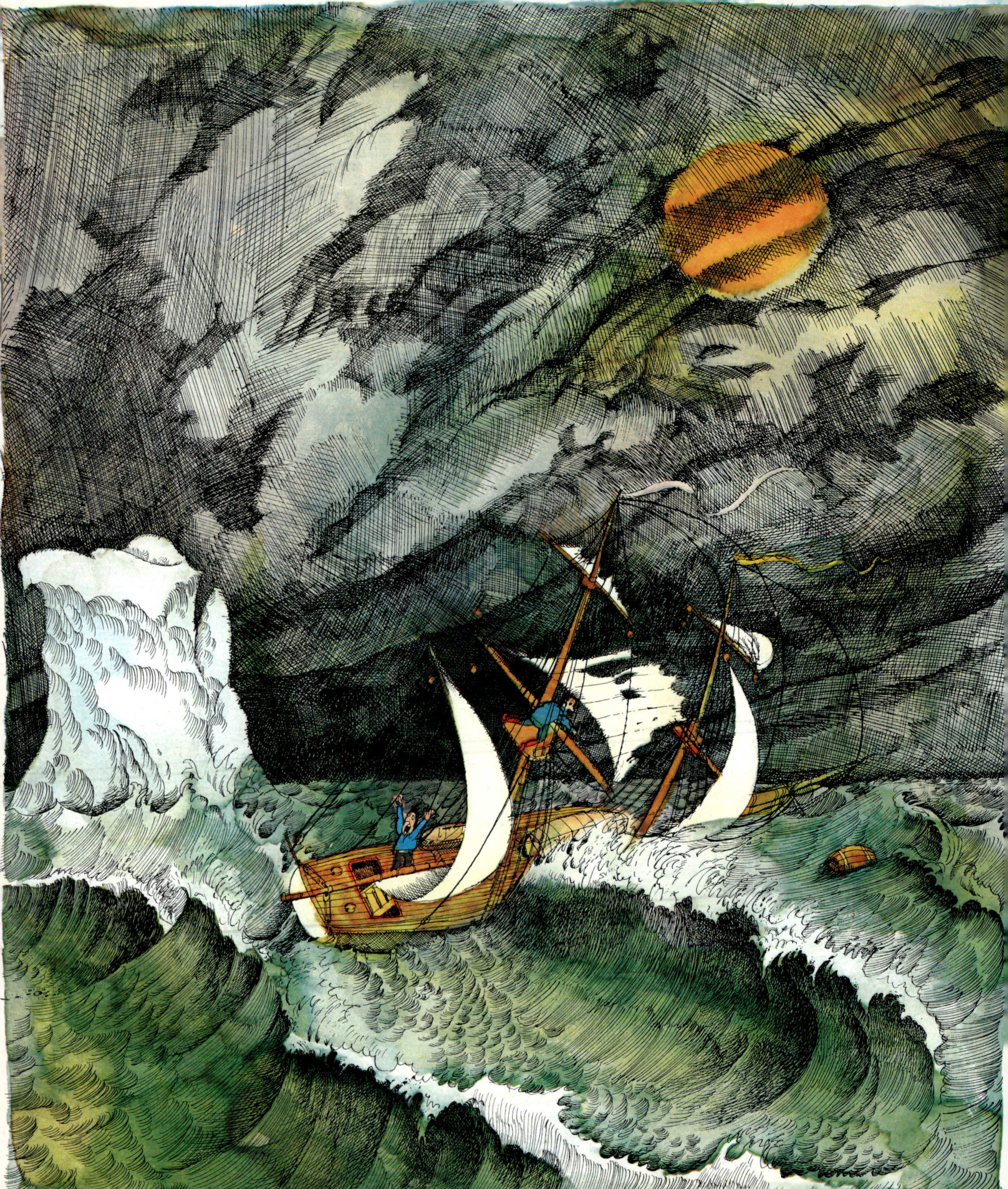

*Length of lifeline packed ready for firing*

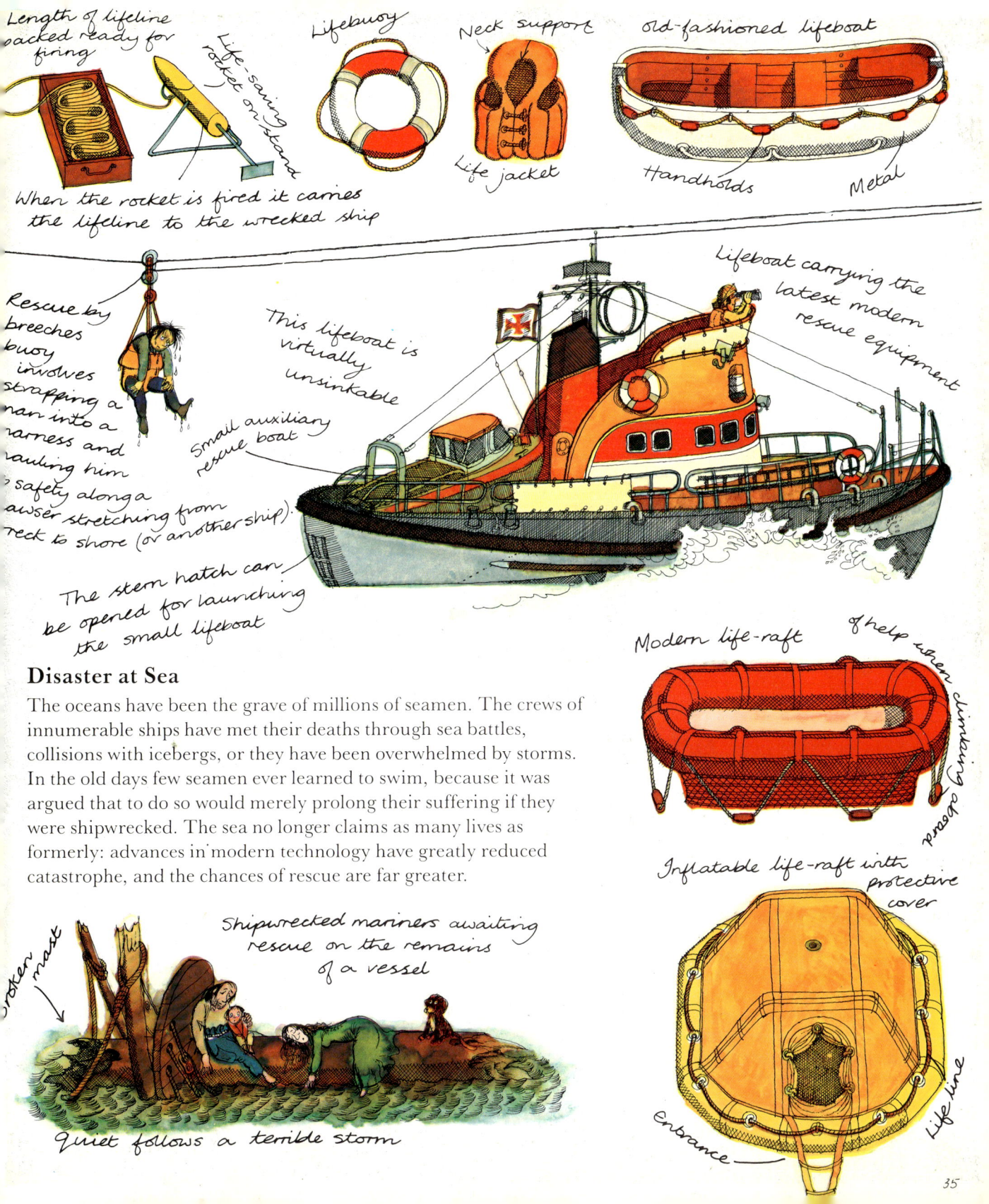

*Life-saving rocket on stand*

*Lifebuoy*

*Neck support*

*Life jacket*

*Old-fashioned lifeboat*

*Handholds*  *Metal*

When the rocket is fired it carries the lifeline to the wrecked ship

Rescue by breeches buoy involves strapping a man into a harness and hauling him to safety along a hawser stretching from wreck to shore (or another ship).

*This lifeboat is virtually unsinkable*

*Small auxiliary rescue boat*

*Lifeboat carrying the latest modern rescue equipment*

The stern hatch can be opened for launching the small lifeboat

*Modern life-raft*

*of help when climbing aboard*

*Inflatable life-raft with protective cover*

*entrance*  *lifeline*

## Disaster at Sea

The oceans have been the grave of millions of seamen. The crews of innumerable ships have met their deaths through sea battles, collisions with icebergs, or they have been overwhelmed by storms. In the old days few seamen ever learned to swim, because it was argued that to do so would merely prolong their suffering if they were shipwrecked. The sea no longer claims as many lives as formerly: advances in modern technology have greatly reduced catastrophe, and the chances of rescue are far greater.

*Shipwrecked mariners awaiting rescue on the remains of a vessel*

*Broken mast*

Quiet follows a terrible storm

# Fishing

The world's rich fishing grounds have encouraged a great many different methods of fishing. Among the most daring fishermen are the Kwakiutl Indians of western Canada who catch whales from their canoes, using hand-held harpoons which they thrust or hurl into the animal's body. Their reckless bravery can only be appreciated by those who have actually seen them hunt — for a whale in its death throes is a formidable adversary.

For thousands of years fish were so

*Marker buoy*
*Weight*
*Cork floats*
*Gill net*

Many different kinds of traps are used for catching fish: the fish readily find their way into the trap but are unable to get out again.

*Bait (usually fish roes)*
*Tapering ends*
*Simple fish trap (kept open by wooden hoops)*
*Trawl (cod end)*
*Mouth of the net*

Trawl: the trawl is a tapered bag made from netting which is towed through the water. The mesh allows the water to escape but not the fish.

An accurately placed trawl can catch an entire shoal of herrings

Two herrings which since their youth have been of an independent turn of mind

*Jib* *Mainsail* *Mizzen*
*Trawler with jib, mainsail and mizzen*
*Dinghy*
*Wooden float*
*Marker buoy*
*Anchor*
*Ground line* *Snood* *Fish hook*

Long line with marker buoys, used in fishing for halibut

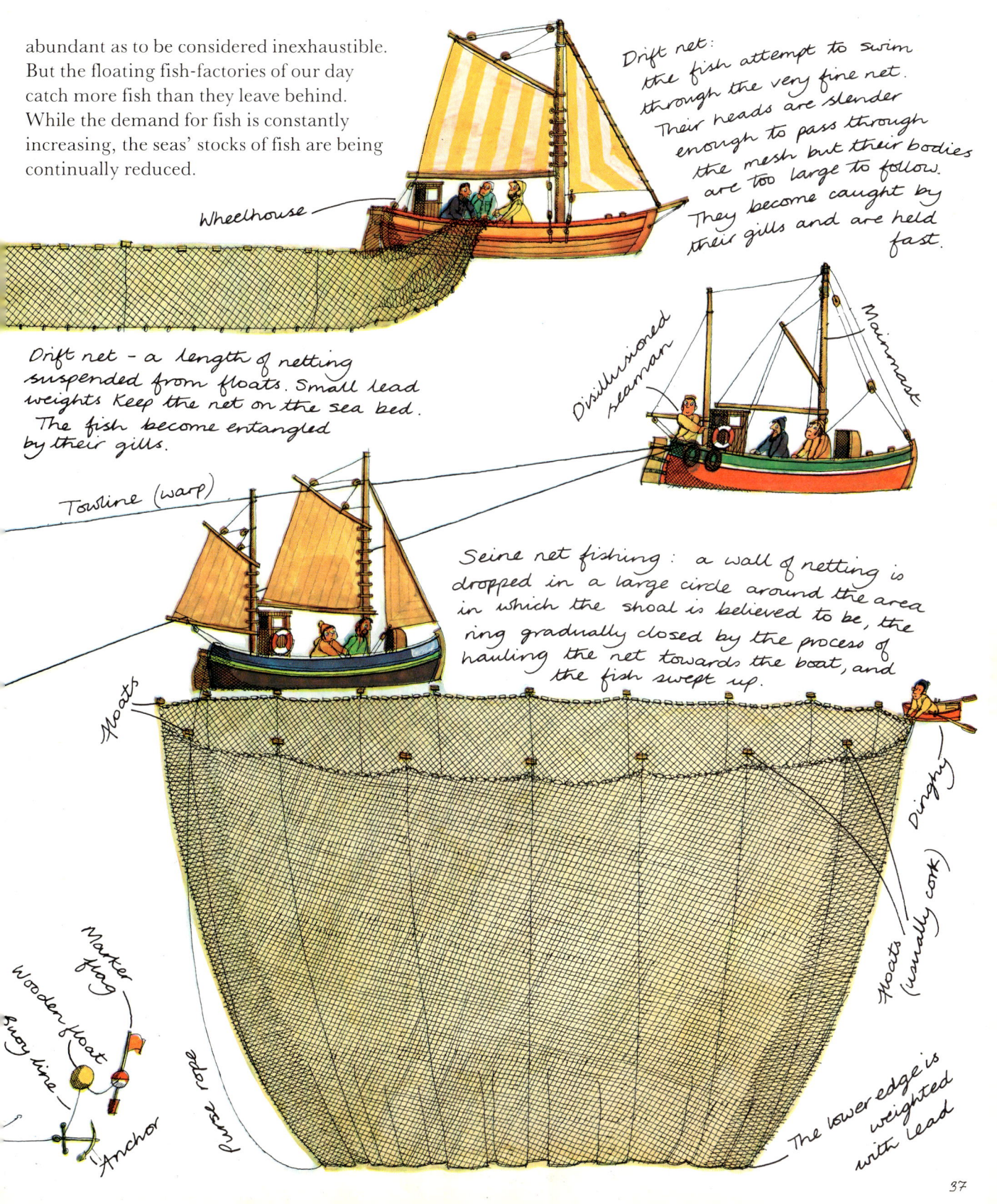

abundant as to be considered inexhaustible. But the floating fish-factories of our day catch more fish than they leave behind. While the demand for fish is constantly increasing, the seas' stocks of fish are being continually reduced.

Wheelhouse

Drift net: the fish attempt to swim through the very fine net. Their heads are slender enough to pass through the mesh but their bodies are too large to follow. They become caught by their gills and are held fast.

Drift net – a length of netting suspended from floats. Small lead weights keep the net on the sea bed. The fish become entangled by their gills.

Disillusioned seaman

Mainmast

Towline (warp)

Seine net fishing: a wall of netting is dropped in a large circle around the area in which the shoal is believed to be, the ring gradually closed by the process of hauling the net towards the boat, and the fish swept up.

Floats

Dinghy

Floats (usually cork)

The lower edge is weighted with lead

Marker flag

Wooden float

Buoy line

Anchor

Purse rope

37

The whale's nostrils are on the top of its head. As it breathes, a mixture of air and water vapour is squirted out through its blowhole

Greenland right whale

Massive tail (flukes)

Octopus

Tentacles

Suckers

Shark

Triangular dorsal fin

Shoal of herrings

Sardines

Tunnyfish

Modern whale catcher

opening through which whales are hauled up a ramp to the deck

Factory ship (supporting a covey of catchers)

## Whaling

Whaling has always been an occupation undertaken only by extremely tough and courageous men. Until about a century ago whales were hunted from open rowing boats with hand-held harpoons. (Harpoons are lances with barbed tips, and are attached by a long coil of rope to the boat.) Fragile whale boats were frequently smashed to matchwood, and many a whaler was killed by his badly wounded quarry.

The invention of the harpoon gun and the development of ocean-going catchers greatly improved the efficiency of whaling to the extent that several species of whales are now threatened with extinction.

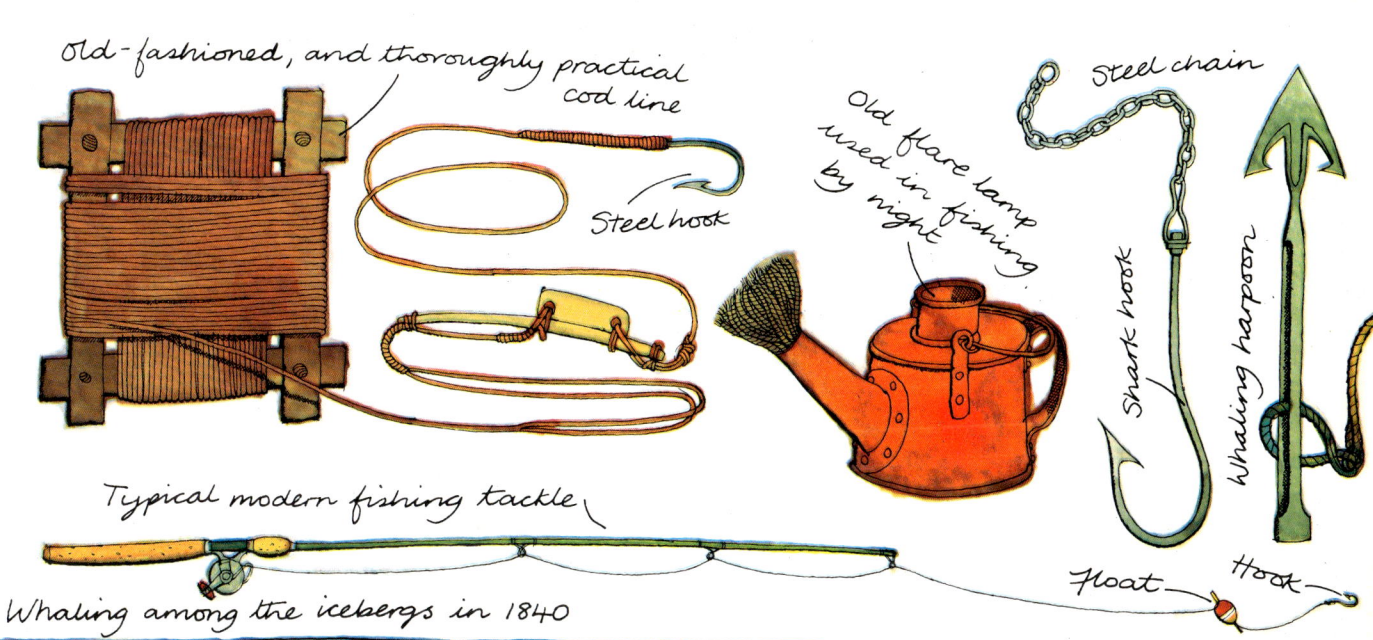

Old-fashioned, and thoroughly practical cod line

Steel hook

Old flare lamp used in fishing by night

Steel chain

Shark hook

Whaling harpoon

Typical modern fishing tackle

Float    Hook

Whaling among the icebergs in 1840

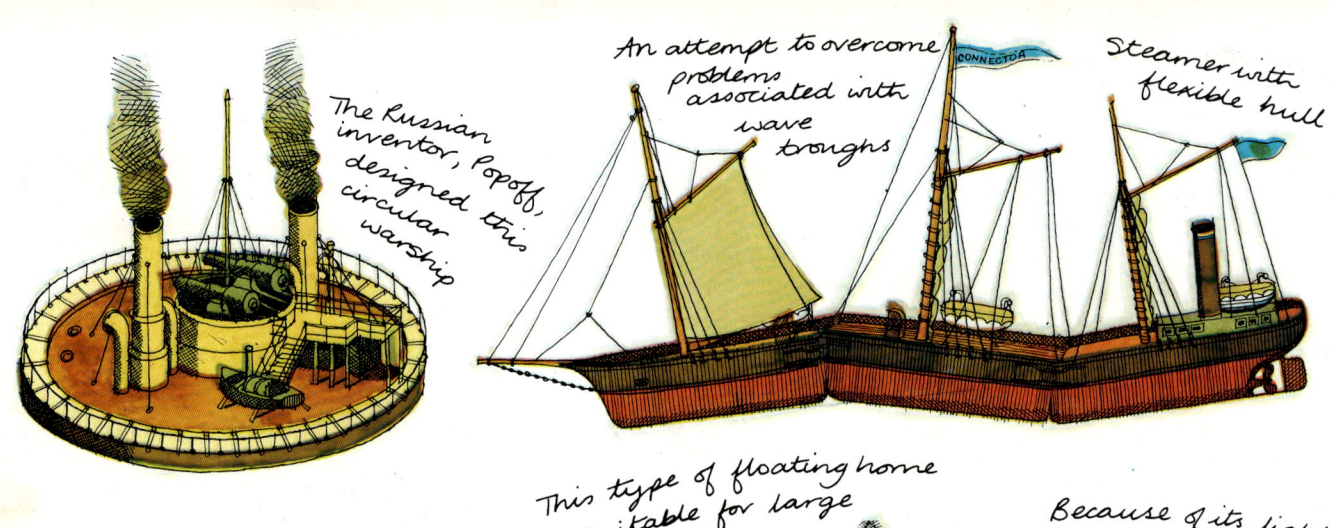

The Russian inventor, Popoff, designed this circular warship

An attempt to overcome problems associated with wave troughs

Steamer with flexible hull

This pedal-taxi plied for hire on romantic lakes

The driver was concealed behind a wooden swan

This type of floating home is suitable for large ports and harbours and slow-flowing rivers

Known as a boat house

Because of its light weight the rubber dinghy can be easily transported, which makes it particularly suitable for bathing and life-saving.

Fuel container

Mooring buoy

The infant Moses floating in his rush basket

An attempt to transport rafts of timber across the Atlantic from the forested areas of North America to Europe. Gales, storms and rough seas made this idea impracticable.

Twin hulls are joined together to form a single boat

Racing catamaran

Trapeze

Seamen have long practised the art of building miniature sailing ships — and even mountains and villages — by inserting pieces through the narrow necks of bottles

Ship in a bottle

In order to put an end to senseless (and increasing competitive) ostentation, one of the doges of Venice prohibited the use of gold or colours on gondolas. To this day all Venetian gondolas are black.

40

**Water skier** — The boat's momentum enables the skier to remain on the surface.

**Surfboard** — Surfing calls for great skill and physical fitness.

This four-man racing boat (shell), known as a coxless four, is used in competitive rowing.

Rudder — Stroke — Oar

The German, Dr. Lindemann, sitting in the collapsible boat in which he crossed the Atlantic.

**Foldboat**

Pilot — Radio direction finder

An aircraft catapulted from the passenger liner 'Bremen' in mid-Atlantic enabled mail to reach New York two days earlier than would otherwise have been possible.

Clippers were sailing ships designed for speed. Longer and narrower than ordinary sailing vessels, their reputation stemmed from the incredibly short time they took to cross the Atlantic. Among other things they transported European prospectors to the Californian goldfields.

Drawer-clipper

**Clipper** — The so-called tea-clippers were engaged in the China tea trade during the 19th century. Competition was intense.

One of the most famous of them all, the *Cutty Sark*, averaged 80½ days outward and 82½ homeward.

This hovercraft is designed to travel over water, but it can equally well travel over open stretches of sand or other flat surfaces.

W. Bauer designed this system of windmills for sailing against the wind.

Dinghy

It floats just above the surface

Lightships are floating lighthouses

ELBE 2

Light buoy
Whistling buoy
Bell buoy

The icebreaker has specially strengthened bows for cutting channels through ice.

Strengthened steel plates

Satiated holidaymaker and pedal boat at a small bathing resort

Deep-sea fishing boat
Captain
Old hand

Motorboat
Protective helmet

At speed the boat rises almost clear of the water

Beam of 75 m.

This supertanker carries 300,000 tons of oil

Twin steam turbines generate 37,400 h.p. Crewmen use bicycles to get around the forecastle.

42

**Container ship** — A specialized container ship designed to carry up to 1500 containers, each the size of a railway wagon. The containers are carried in the holds and on deck and are lifted in and out by crane, often being transferred to barges, lighters, trains or lorries for transporting to their final destination.

Hydrofoils achieve high speed by raising the hull clear of the water

Low water resistance

## Specialized Ships

This spread shows a small selection from the immense family of ships. Today, hundreds of different kinds of vessels are designed for highly specialized purposes. The multitude of types is as varied as the purposes they serve, and the design is often complex.

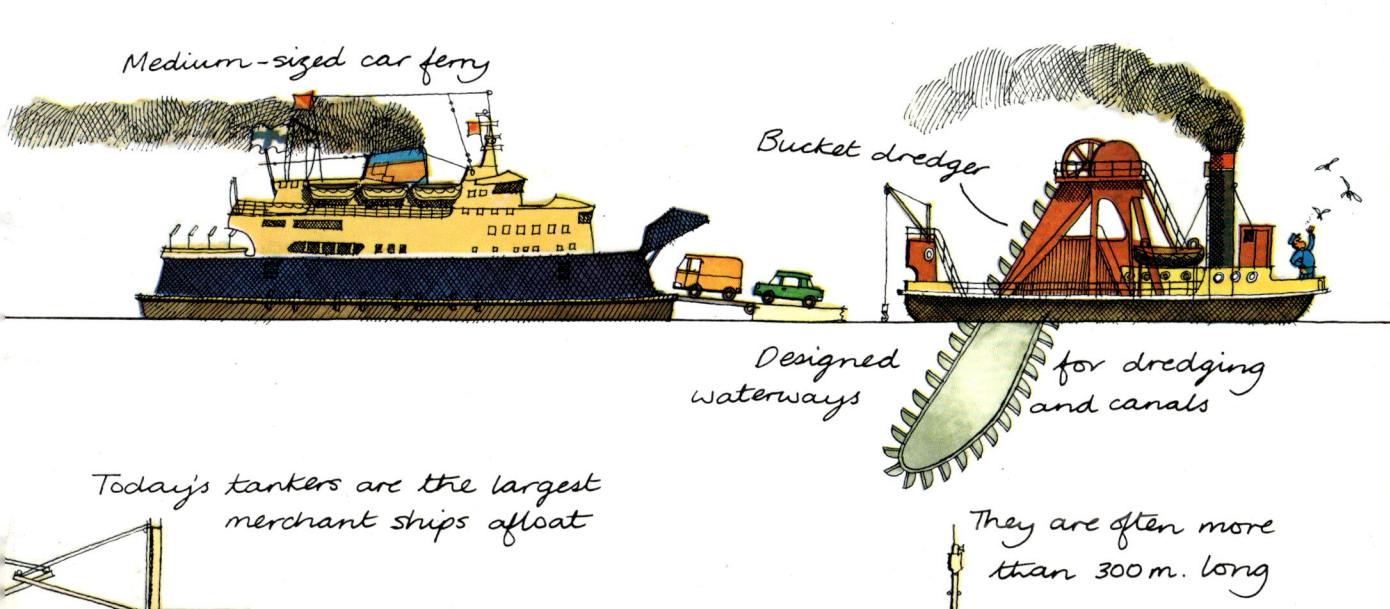

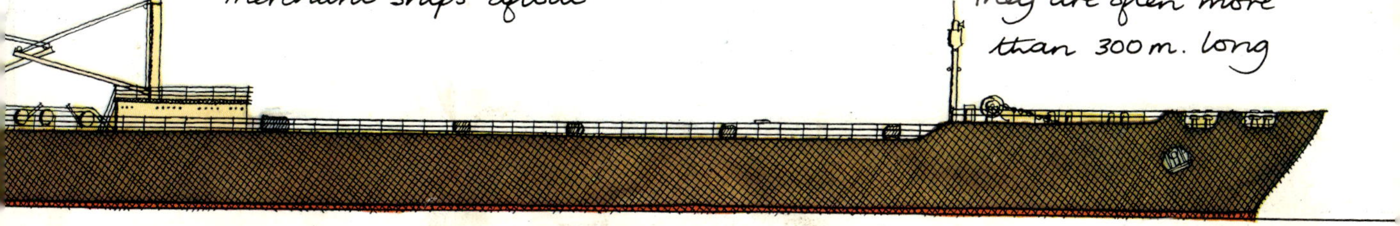

Medium-sized car ferry

Bucket dredger

Designed waterways for dredging and canals

Today's tankers are the largest merchant ships afloat

They are often more than 300 m. long

132 m. long, 4650 sq. m. sail area

The 'Preussen' was the largest full-rigged sailing ship ever built.

Both her hull and her masts were of steel.

She was built in 1902

The 'Mauretania' was one of the most successful passenger liners ever to sail the oceans. She captured and held the Blue Riband of the Atlantic for many years.

Her turbines generated 70,000 h.p.

Launched 1906

The 'France' is the last survivor from the age of the luxury floating palace. She plied the Atlantic route and could accommodate more guests than New York's Astoria Hotel.

Built 1962; still working in 1975

1,112 man crew

Cheap and rapid Atlantic flights in jumbo jets spelt the end of the ocean liner.

44

# A Modern Tug

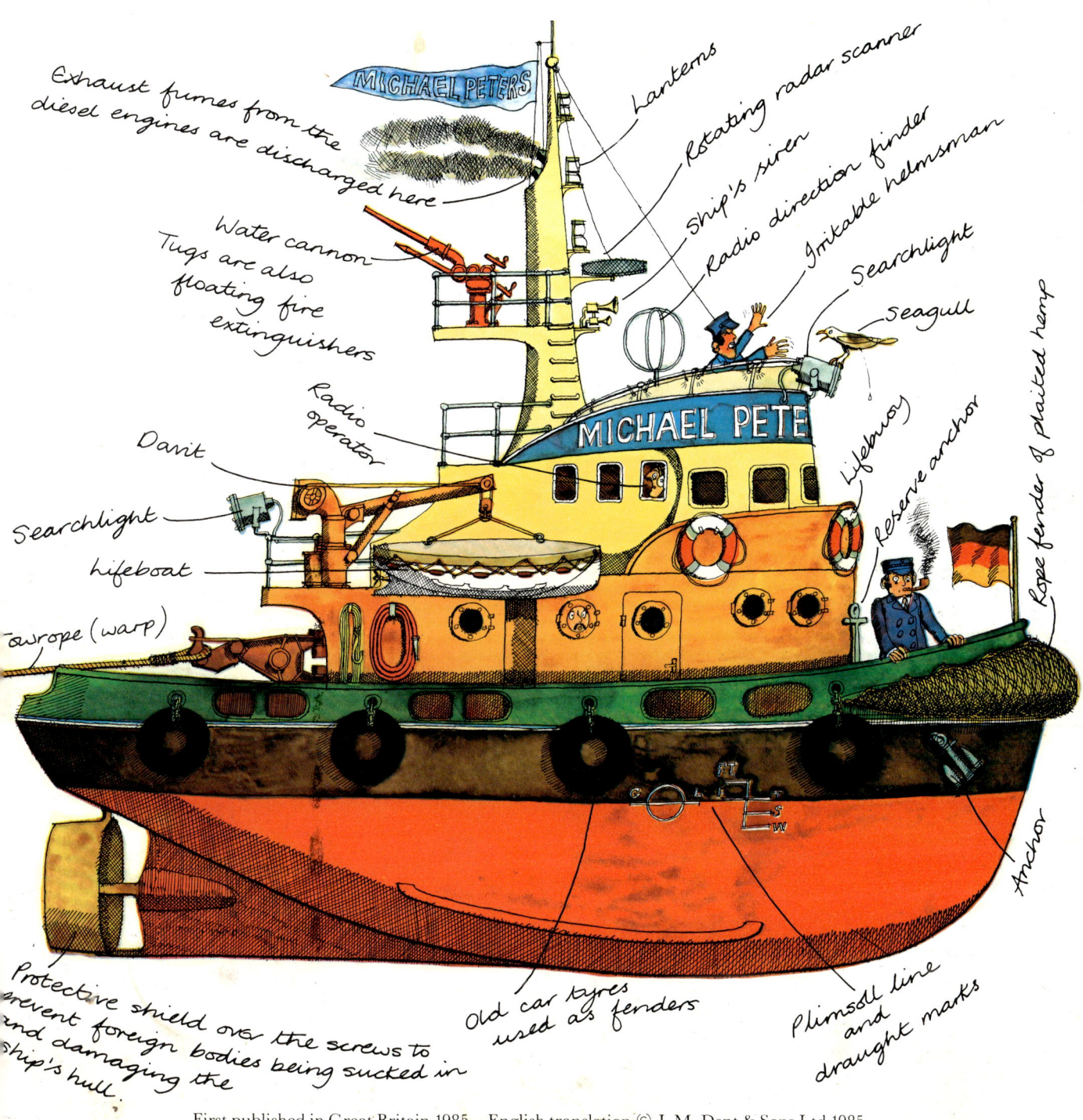

- Exhaust fumes from the diesel engines are discharged here
- Water cannon Tugs are also floating fire extinguishers
- Lanterns
- Rotating radar scanner
- Ship's siren
- Radio direction finder
- Irritable helmsman
- Searchlight
- Seagull
- Radio operator
- Lifebuoy
- Reserve anchor
- Rope fender of plaited hemp
- Davit
- Searchlight
- Lifeboat
- Towrope (warp)
- Protective shield over the screws to prevent foreign bodies being sucked in and damaging the ship's hull
- Old car tyres used as fenders
- Plimsoll line and draught marks
- Anchor

First published in Great Britain 1985   English translation © J. M. Dent & Sons Ltd 1985
Originally published in German under the title *Rund Ums Schiff*   © 1977, 1985 by Otto Maier Verlag, Ravensburg
All rights reserved   Printed in Italy   ISBN 0 460 06230 1